BP PORTRAIT AWARD 2008

BP PORTRAIT AWARD 2008

National Portrait Gallery

Published in Great Britain by
National Portrait Gallery Publications,
National Portrait Gallery,
St Martin's Place, London WC2H 0HE

Published to accompany
the BP Portrait Award 2008,
held at the National Portrait Gallery, London
from 12 June to 14 September 2008,
Wolverhampton Art Gallery
from 27 September to 14 November 2008,
and at the Aberdeen Art Gallery
from 29 November 2008 to 24 January 2009.

For a complete catalogue
of current publications
please write to the address above,
or visit our website at
www.npg.org.uk/publications

ISBN 978-1-85514-394-4

A catalogue record for this book
is available from the British Library.

Publishing Manager: Celia Joicey
Editorial: Claudia Bloch
Design: Anne Sørensen
Production Manager: Ruth Müller-Wirth
Photography: Prudence Cuming
Travel Award photography:
Prudence Cuming and Lorna Mcparland
Printed and bound in Italy

Cover: *Konjit* by Maryam Foroozanfar

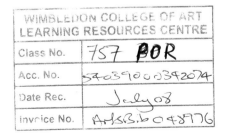

bp

DIRECTOR'S FOREWORD

The two days of judging for the BP Portrait Award 2008 were an exacting process. Starting with the original portraits, the judges examined a total of 1,727 (without knowing the identity of the artists). Retaining some 300 works for their combination of skill and originality, the judges reduced these to about 100 on the second day. Having decided on the overall prize-winners, a final choice was made of fifty-five works for the exhibition.

Whereas the general process of curating exhibitions involves building up a choice of works, the BP Portrait Award is a process of letting go. The judges must agree the final list. In one sense portraits make this straightforward – they are all depictions of individual human subjects. However, the works vary from scrupulously rendered photo-realism to loose expressionist forms, with every manner of brushwork, format and colour range in between. Given that the subjects are not generally known to the judges, the vitality of the rendering of the sitter becomes important, as do items depicted from their lives alongside allegorical or other symbolic elements. The sense of feeling that the subject was present is essential, but there is of course no stipulation of how this engagement between artist and sitter should be translated into the final completed portrait.

Portraiture in Britain and around the world grows in health and invention year on year. While it develops as a genre in its own right, it also intersects with contemporary art – which is itself engaged with issues of identity and representation. The best portraits emerge from an open competition through high quality submission, good management and rigourous judging. I am enormously grateful to BP for their continued support for the BP Portrait Award, comprising competition, exhibition and Travel Award. The continued partnership is an example of sponsorship providing great public benefit in London and around the UK. My warm thanks go to the company and to Tony Hayward, Group Chief Executive.

SANDY NAIRNE
Director, National Portrait Gallery

SPONSOR'S FOREWORD

The National Portrait Gallery is home to the world's largest collection of portraits and BP is delighted to support the BP Portrait Award, which attracts artists from all around the world.

We have supported the BP Portrait Award since 1990, and last year's broadening of the age range gives more people the opportunity to take part in the competition. This year attracted 1,727 entries from twenty-six countries.

I would like to thank everyone at the National Portrait Gallery in making the BP Portrait Award such a success. I would also like to thank the many artists who enter. This includes not only those who are selected for the exhibition, but also the many others who responded to the 'call for entries' and who took the time and perseverance to create a unique portrait painting. It is their enthusiasm which has allowed the BP Portrait Award to grow over the years and increase in popularity.

I am delighted with this year's exhibition as well as the winners of the major Award, the Young Artist Award and the two Travel Awards. I hope you will enjoy and appreciate them as much as my colleagues and I at BP.

TONY HAYWARD
Group Chief Executive, BP

PORTRAITURE

This afternoon, before sitting down to write this essay, I saw a portrait. It was in a small antique shop in Edinburgh. My wife had seen something that interested her, and we had entered the shop showing the usual caution that one needs to exercise in entering such places – one wrong step can bring down a cascade of objects, most of them breakable, some of them pointed. I looked up and there, on the topmost shelf, was a large portrait of a man in early middle age, wearing a suit that dated the picture to somewhere around the middle of the twentieth century. The face was a benign one, somewhat pleased with itself, bespectacled, and with that look which said *successful small businessman*. The proprietor of the shop noticed my interest. 'He had four wives,' he said. 'And a painting and decorating business.' I wondered whether I had missed the clues within the painting, but no. 'His family told us about the four wives,' said the proprietor, 'when we cleared the house'.

This snatch of conversation, inconsequential though it may be, reveals something about portraits and how we respond to them. There were other paintings in the shop – of ships on the Forth, banal landscapes and so on – but this painting was the one to which my eye was ineluctably drawn. I had immediately found myself not only asking who the subject was, but answering the question before the proprietor had the chance to enlighten me. He was a local businessman, I had decided; a member of his fair share of committees, somebody whose life ran correctly and uneventfully to the grave. I was right about some of these particulars; I was wrong about his personal life. Unless he had the misfortune to lose a number of his wives to natural causes, being married four times suggested a roving eye. And with that knowledge, the portrait became much more interesting.

But there was another matter of interest in all this. His family had *sold* him, and that told us something about them – they had no attic. People are often reluctant to dispose of portraits of their forbears; there is something impious about selling the portrait of one's

REVEREND ROBERT
WALKER SKATING ON
DUDDINGSTON LOCH
1755–1808
Sir Henry Raeburn, c.1795
Oil on canvas
762 x 635mm
(30 x 25")
National Gallery
of Scotland

grandfather. Painted portraits still have a totemic significance. At a primitive level they are a link with the subject – they represent him or her in the same way as that in which the relic connects the faithful with the departed saint, or the voodoo doll stands for an intended victim. So when a tyrant falls, his portrait naturally becomes the symbolic target of those whom he oppressed. In our own times we have seen this vividly demonstrated in images of people venting their rage on the statues and portraits of deposed dictators. This should not surprise us. Every student of art learns that portraits are used for social and ideological purposes, often with an effect that is the exact opposite of what was intended by the propagandist.

An antique shop is one place where one might come across a portrait, but there are many others. Portraiture is all around us, at every stage in our lives. It is there in the primary school – in the coloured pencil drawings pinned to the walls, the portraits of mother as a stick-woman in front of an idealized house with a smoking chimney, beneath a friendly sun. It is there in the buildings in which we later study and work – universities and colleges are full of portraits, largely ignored by the students – and of course it is there in profusion if we seek it out in museums and galleries. And yet in spite of the ubiquity of portraiture, many take it for granted, or even treat it as the poor relation of other forms of painting. Sale-room prices tell an interesting story. While contemporary art attracts often quite staggering prices at auction, exquisitely executed portraits by well-known painters will usually go for a fraction of those prices. Eighteenth-century portraits by Sir Henry Raeburn or George Romney may go for the price of a car, while favoured contemporary artists may go for the cost of a house, and a substantial one at that. Naturally there will be some blurring of this distinction. The portraits of Francis Bacon, Lucian Freud or David Hockney are in the upper reaches of the art market, and a good Gainsborough will still be the subject of stiff competition, but in general portraiture seems to be out of fashion with collectors. This must be a matter of regret, not only because it diminishes the importance of a profoundly important branch of painting, but because it might discourage young artists from entering the field. At least the BP Portrait Award helps to redress that balance.

As a supporter of portraiture and a very modest collector of portraits, I have often wondered why it is that portrait painters have had to struggle for their place in the pantheon. One of the reasons may be a particular view of what the portrait is. Perhaps there is a feeling that portraiture lacks the universality of other forms of painting. It may be seen as specific and focused, designed to remind us simply of how people looked. Obviously this is a very limited view, but one can understand why it is held. The genesis of the portrait is indeed often very personal – an artist is commissioned to do a portrait of a particular subject for the benefit of

LUCIAN FREUD
b.1922
Lucian Freud, 1963
Oil on canvas
305 x 251mm
(12 x 9⅞")
National Portrait Gallery
(NPG 5205)

that subject, or of persons close to him or her. The artist who paints a landscape or still life is not addressing a closed circle of people, but any person who may later look upon that painting. There is nothing private about such a painting. It is intended to speak to whomsoever contemplates it. By contrast, there may be an assumption that the portrait of a named person is not addressed to us; it is intended for those who appreciated or knew the subject. We feel almost as if we are intruding.

This sense of the privacy of the portrait is not as strong if the portrait is represented as a generic picture. As I write this, on a wall behind me there hangs a pencil sketch by Scottish artist James Cowie (1886–1956). Called *Portrait of a Boy*, it is a fine example of Cowie's skill as a draughtsman. I wonder if my view of this picture would be any different were it to be called *Portrait of John*, or *Portrait of John Macdonald*. I suspect

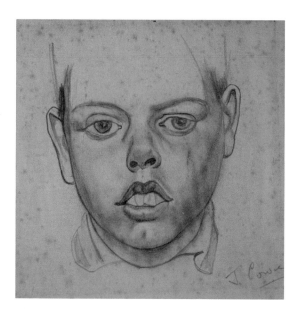

PORTRAIT OF A BOY
James Cowie, 1920s
Drawing on paper
152 x 152mm
(6 x 6")
Private Collection

that our reactions to the portrait are subtly changed by the degree of personalisation. Do we want to hang on our walls the portrait of a person whom we do not know personally? The answer is probably no – unless there is a sufficient distance between us and the subject. I would not wish to have a portrait of, say, a prominent contemporary politician on my wall unless I knew him or admired him for some reason. But I would have no objection to a portrait of a grandee of the seventeenth century, because I can hardly assert any familiarity with such a person. Similarly, a portrait of a named person by a very highly regarded contemporary painter will be considered intrinsically interesting because the subject is eclipsed by the artist. A portrait by a celebrated artist will probably be seen as being first and foremost about the artist rather than his subject.

Great portraiture, of course, transcends the personal. The portraits selected for the BP Portrait Award 2008, for the most part, will have been chosen not because they are of subjects known to the public, but because of what they say about humanity. That is not to say that the subject is irrelevant. The sitter is crucial, not just as that person but as what that person represents. A portrait may be as powerful as any allegorical painting in what it says about what it is to be human; about our vulnerability, our hopes and ambitions. What each of the portraits in this collection will do is to say 'here is a person', and 'this is what it is to be that person'.

When I look at a portrait, I am drawn first to the eyes, because it is there that one sees the essence of the subject. That establishes the contact. I then go on to look for some detail in the clothing or the background which says something more general about humanity. This involves a very particular scrutiny, and it is one which I suspect comes from being a novelist.

In common with many writers, I do not give detailed descriptions of the appearance of my characters. I do, however, rely a great deal on descriptions of perhaps one item, of clothing or of some personal possession, to say what I want to say about what the character represents. For example, in my Botswana novels, the *No. 1 Ladies' Detective Agency* books, I try to say a lot about Mma Ramotswe's assistant, Mma Makutsi, through her possessions. We know that she has large glasses and problem skin – that is all that is said about how she looks. But we know, too, that she has a lace handkerchief of which she is very fond and which is becoming threadbare. This handkerchief stands for her desire to escape poverty; it stands for her efforts to make something of her life. Rather a lot for a small handkerchief to do but it works, I hope. And then there are her shoes, of which she is inordinately proud. Shoes can be such poignant objects – one of the most horrifying images of the dark side of the twentieth century is that haunting photograph of shoes belonging to Second World War victims of the gas chambers, shoe piled upon shoe. The image says more about that immense human tragedy than thousands of words of description.

The clothing in portraits, then, speaks eloquently and poignantly of how we would like others to see us,

AN OLD MAN AND A BOY
Domenico Ghirlandaio,
1480s
Oil on panel
627 x 463mm
(24⁵/₈ x 18¹/₄")
Louvre, Paris

of what we would like to be, of what we actually are. A portrait of a person who has dressed up as best as he or she can may be very moving, because it shows us that we all want to be loved, we all want to be taken seriously, we all want to be something other than the vulnerable transient creatures that we are.

This moral function of portraiture – a reminder of our shared humanity – would by itself be sufficient reason for portraiture's celebration. But there is so much more. In particular, the portrait lends itself to the portrayal of beauty. There are ugly portraits, of course, but these are not necessarily portraits of human ugliness. *An Old Man and a Boy* by Domenico Ghirlandaio (1449–94) shows a man with a grossly bulbous nose looking down upon a perfect child. Both are beautiful, though; the man with his ugly nose and the child with his flaxen locks. And this, I think, applies to so many portraits. Even those who are not conventionally physically blessed may appear beautiful in a portrait. Indeed, a good portrait painter will find beauty in any subject, because there is a sense, surely, in which the human face will always appear beautiful, caught in the right pose, seen in the right light, understood in the right way.

We are bombarded today with photographic images of the human face and the human body. This can make us forget that the face and body reflect the drama and possibilities of our lives, as well as reminding us of those emotions and thoughts that make for a full, considered life. Painted portraiture provides a calm moment in which we can think about just these things. It helps us, I believe, to be more appreciative, more forgiving, and ultimately kinder.

ALEXANDER MCCALL SMITH
Novelist

BP PORTRAIT AWARD 2008

The Portrait Award, in its twenty-ninth year at the National Portrait Gallery and its nineteenth year of sponsorship by BP, is an annual event aimed at encouraging artists to focus upon and develop the theme of portraiture in their work. The competition is open to everyone aged eighteen and over, in recognition of the outstanding and innovative work currently being produced by artists of all ages working in portraiture.

THE JUDGES

Chair: Sandy Nairne, Director, National Portrait Gallery

Sadie Coles, Director, Sadie Coles HQ

David Mach RA, artist

Corinne Miller, Head of Arts and Museums, Wolverhampton

Des Violaris, Director, UK Arts & Culture, BP

THE PRIZES

The BP Portrait Awards are:

First Prize
£25,000, plus at the Gallery's discretion a commission worth £4,000 to paint a well-known person

Second Prize
£8,000

Third Prize
£6,000

BP Young Artist Award
£5,000

PRIZE-WINNING PORTRAITS

PORTRAIT OF AMANDA SMITH AT VINCENT AVENUE
Simon Davis
Oil on board, 650 x 398mm (25⅝ x 15⅝")

UNTITLED
Peiyuan Jiang
Oil and acrylic on canvas, 700 x 800mm (27$\frac{1}{2}$ x 31$\frac{1}{2}$")

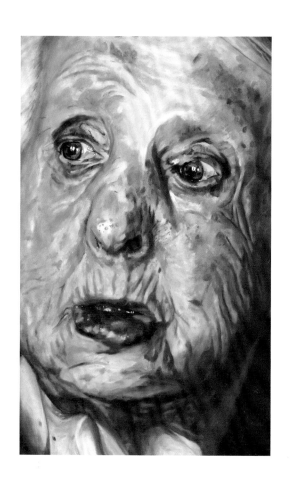

HANNAH O'BRIEN
Robert O'Brien
Oil on board, 300 x 200mm (11³/₄ x 7⁷/₈")

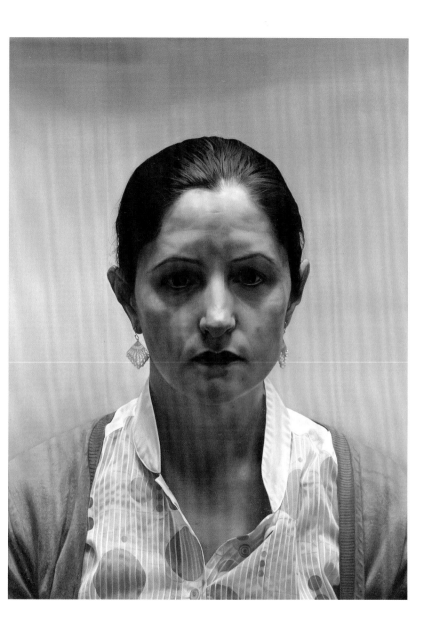

K
Craig Wylie
Oil on canvas, 2100 x 1650mm (82⁵⁄₈ x 65")

SELECTED PORTRAITS

MELANIE
Jackie Anderson
Oil on cotton on board, 1020 x 1200mm (40$^{1}/_{8}$ x 47$^{1}/_{4}$")

LAURA
Andres Basurto
Oil on linen, 360 x 280mm (14$^{1}/_{8}$ x 11")

HEAD-SP4
John Beard
Oil on linen, 1800 x 1800mm (70$^7/_8$ x 70$^7/_8$")

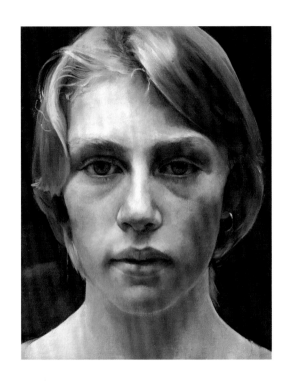

SERAPH
Celia Bennett
Oil on canvas on board, 380 x 300mm (15 x 11³/₄")

BLUE POOL (DATUK VINOD SEKHAR FAMILY)
Paul Benney
Oil on canvas, 1800 x 1200mm (70$^{7}/_{8}$ x 47$^{1}/_{4}$")

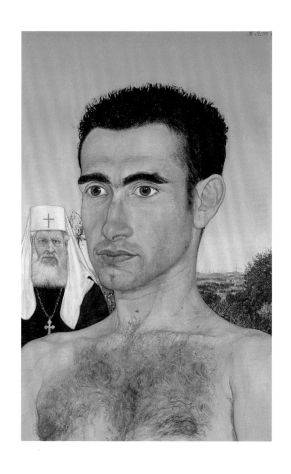

PORTRAIT OF A SERBIAN STUDENT OF THEOLOGY
WITH SERBIAN PATRIARCH IN BACKROUND
Emmanouil Bitsakis
Oil on canvas, 330 x 210mm (13 x 8¼")

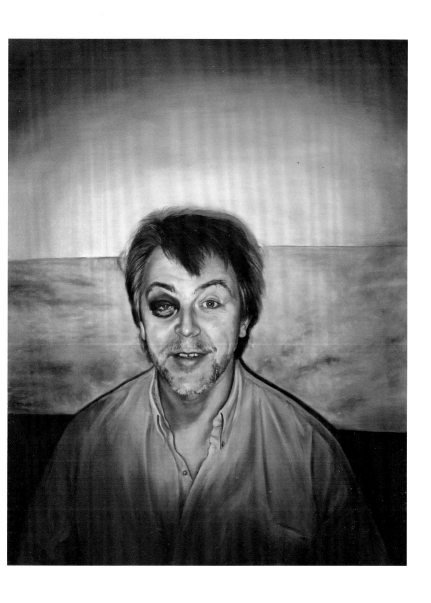

SUNNY JIM
Sue Burns
Oil on canvas, 1420 x 1115mm (55^{7}/$_{8}$ x 43^{7}/$_{8}$")

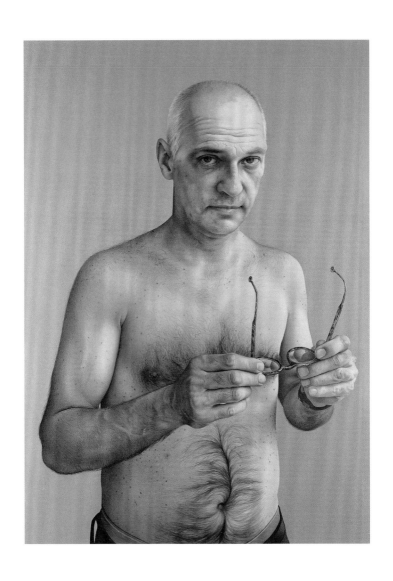

BIRTHMARKS AND CHEST HAIR
Annemarie Busschers
Acrylic on canvas, 2500 x 1600mm (98³/₈ x 63")

OOH ERR MRS!
Stephen Chappell
Oil on canvas, 760 x 610mm (29^{7}/$_{8}$ x 24")

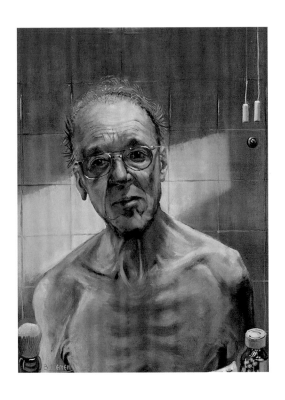

IN THE BATHROOM MIRROR
Brian Clements
Oil on board, 460 x 360mm (18¹/₈ x 14¹/₈")

JOHN
Benjamin Cohen
Oil on canvas, 2000 x 1490mm (78³/₄ x 58⁵/₈")

HER NAME IS RIO
Lucie Cookson
Oil on canvas, 700 x 1100mm (27$^{1}/_{2}$ x 43$^{1}/_{4}$")

34

METAMORPHOSIS
José Luis Corella García
Oil on wooden board, 1000 x 1000mm (39³/₈ x 39³/₈")

WORDTOMOTHER
Arth Daniels
Oil on canvas, 970 x 1370mm (38$^{1}/_{4}$ x 53$^{7}/_{8}$")

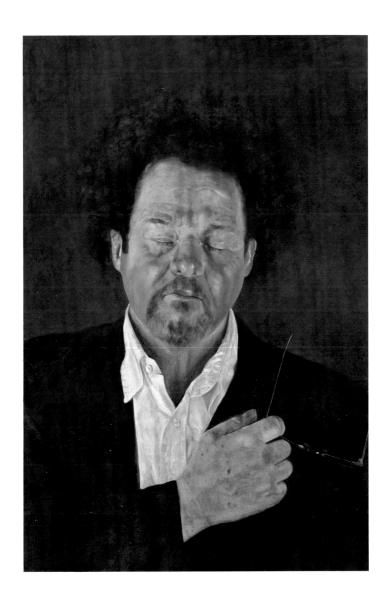

MIKE FIGGIS
Nerys Davies
Oil on canvas, 1524 x 1016mm (60 x 40")

MOSS BANK
Tom Dewhurst
Oil on canvas, 1020 x 770mm (40$\frac{1}{8}$ x 30$\frac{3}{8}$")

DAD AND HIS NEWSPAPER
Alejandro Domingo
Oil on board, 400 x 400mm (15³/₄ x 15³/₄")

KONJIT
Maryam Foroozanfar
Acrylic on canvas, 254 x 203mm (10 x 8")

CARLOS, 27 YEARS LATER
Nina Mae Fowler
Oil on canvas, 300 x 250mm (11³/₄ x 9⁷/₈")

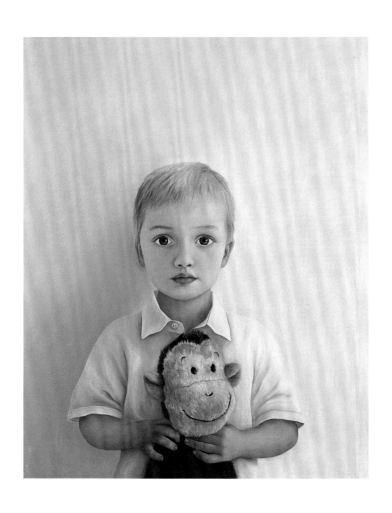

MARK PRICHARD
Nicola Green
Oil on board, 780 x 630mm (30³/₄ x 24³/₄")

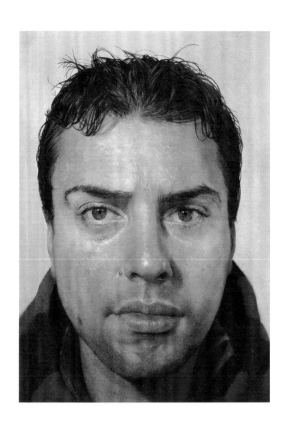

MANUEL
Gabriele Grones
Oil on canvas, 280 x 200mm (11 x 7$\frac{7}{8}$")

CAMISA A CUADROS (CHEQUERED SHIRT)
Pauline Hazelwood
Oil on canvas, 610 x 457mm (24 x 18")

44

LA BOHÈME
Wim Heldens
Oil on canvas, 540 x 660mm (21¹/₄ x 26")

MADE IN BRITAIN
Linda Hubbard
Oil on canvas, 600 x 500mm (23^5/$_8$ x 19^5/$_8$")

SELF PORTRAIT WITH WINNIE
Andrew Hunt
Oil on board, 828 x 587mm (32⁵/₈ x 23¹/₈")

WALTER
Oliver Jeffers
Oil on canvas, 1300 x 1000mm (51$\frac{1}{8}$ x 39$\frac{3}{8}$")

48

LLIANA
Krasimir Kolev
Oil on canvas, 540 x 930mm (21$\frac{1}{4}$ x 36$\frac{5}{8}$")

LOLA
Alison Lee
Oil on canvas, 1020 x 765mm (40^1/$_8$ x 30^1/$_8$")

HAMZAH: THE SILVER PENNY
Paul Lisak
Oil on canvas, 1000 x 950mm (39³/₈ x 37³/₈")

ELIXIR
Barry McGlashan
Oil on wooden panel, 1220 x 615mm (48 x 24¹/₄")

RETRATO DEL PINTOR CARLOS MONDRIÀ
(PORTRAIT OF THE PAINTER CARLOS MONDRIÀ)
Alejandro Marco Montalvo
Oil on wood, 1200 x 900mm (47¼ x 35⅜")

MY MOTHER-IN-LAW, ANNE, AND HER SISTER, AUNTIE AUDREY
Tony Noble
Oil on canvas, 1085 x 910mm (42³/₄ x 35⁷/₈")

TAHA (AS RONIN)
Tim Okamura
Oil on canvas, 1917 x 1371mm (75$\frac{1}{2}$ x 54")

55

SIR JEREMY ISAACS
Tom Phillips CBE RA
Oil on canvas, 1215 x 910mm (47^{7}/$_{8}$ x 35^{7}/$_{8}$")

BUTI
Flavia Maria Pitis
Oil on canvas, 800 x 600mm (31$^1/_2$ x 23$^5/_8$")

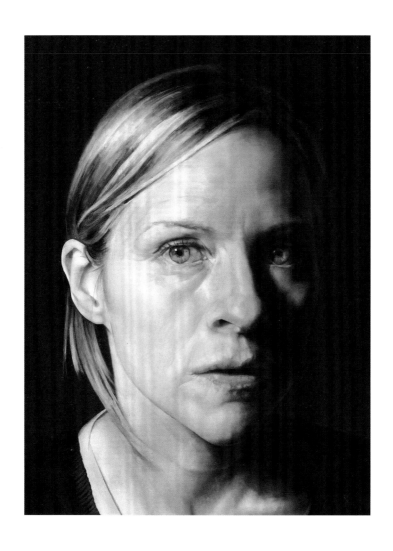

PORTRAIT
Angela Reilly
Oil on canvas, 1016 x 762mm (40 x 30")

KERRY
Keith Robinson
Oil on canvas, 1000 x 755mm (39³/₈ x 29³/₄")

JOHN WATERS (JOURNALIST AND AUTHOR)
Oisin Roche
Oil on canvas, 1702 x 991mm (67 x 39")

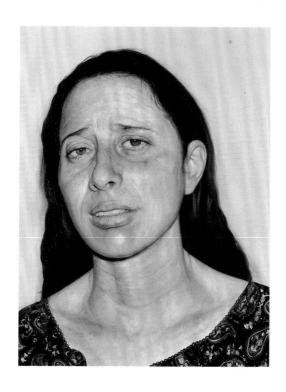

FROM THE SERIES ANSWERED PRAYERS (BRUNA)
Rafael Rodríguez Cruz
Oil on board, 530 x 480mm (20$^7/_8$ x 18$^7/_8$")

MARIAN DORMINT (MARIAN SLEEPING)
Josep Joaquim Santilari Perarnau
Oil on canvas, 270 x 300mm (10^{5}/$_{8}$ x 11^{3}/$_{4}$")

KRISTY, 3RD ATTEMPT
Geert Schless
Oil on wooden board, 250 x 200mm (9$^{7}/_{8}$ x 7$^{7}/_{8}$")

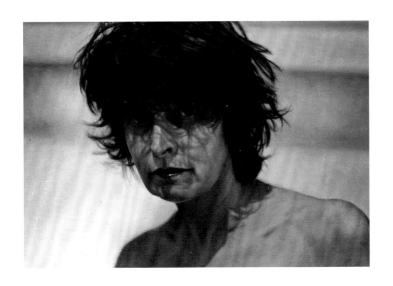

TINA
Fred Schley
Oil on canvas, 240 x 350mm (9$^1/_2$ x 13$^3/_4$")

RACHEL
Elie Shamir
Oil on canvas, 600 x 500mm (23⅝ x 19⅝")

STUDENT DEBT
Nathan Stell
Acrylic on canvas, 615 x 810mm (24¼ x 31⅞")

VOLKER
Benita Stoney
Egg tempera on board, 267 x 218mm (10$^{1}/_{2}$ x 8$^{5}/_{8}$")

ON DUDDERY ROAD
Benjamin Sullivan
Oil on canvas, 680 x 400mm (26³/₄ x 15³/₄"),
1100 x 700mm (43¹/₄ x 27¹/₂"), 680 x 400mm (26³/₄ x 15³/₄")

NATALIE
Jason Walker
Oil on canvas, 711 x 558mm (28 x 22")

PROFESSORS CHRIS AND UTA FRITH
Emma Wesley
Acrylic on board, 1230 x 737mm (48³/₈ x 29")

BOOTS NO.7 (2)
Harriet White
Oil on canvas, 910 x 1220mm (35$^7/_8$ x 48")

SELF
Nigel Wood
Oil on canvas, 450 x 280mm (17³/₄ x 11")

MERAL
Joanna Yates
Oil on canvas, 1000 x 1200mm (39³/₈ x 47¹/₄")

BP TRAVEL AWARD

Each year exhibitors are invited to submit a proposal for the BP Travel Award. The aim of the Award is to give an artist the opportunity to experience working in a different environment, in Britain or abroad, on a project related to portraiture. The artist's work is then shown as part of the following year's BP Portrait Award exhibition and tour.

THE JUDGES 2007 AND 2008

Sarah Howgate, Contemporary Curator,
National Portrait Gallery

Liz Rideal, Art Resource Developer,
National Portrait Gallery

Des Violaris, Director, UK Arts & Culture, BP

THE PRIZE WINNERS 2007

For the first time in its sixteen-year history the BP Travel Award went to two winners in 2007 – Timothy Hyman, who travelled to India to paint a large commemorative group portrait, and Gareth Reid, who spent three weeks travelling around Finland visiting winter-swimming clubs.

Throughout the 1980s I'd been co-opted into a close-knit group of Indian artists, centred on the painter Bhupen Khakhar (1934–2003). In February 2007, after a gap of twelve years, I returned to India for an exhibition, and it was in those few days among old friends, all of us still mourning Bhupen, that I conceived the idea of a commemorative group portrait. This difficult project required preliminary studies of each of the protagonists in different regions of India, and it was suddenly rendered possible by the BP Travel Award a few months later.

AROUND BHUPEN
Timothy Hyman

Delhi, 5 December 2007
I've just unpacked and set up my workspace, when the phone rings; a surprise first-day visit from Dillu who always has plans to turn my life upside down. But she submits to being drawn, sitting cross-legged and smoking, and I enjoy the whole exchange – even if her response when she sees the result is, 'Now I'm really depressed!' I'll draw her again tomorrow. She's off to Goa, so this is my only chance.

Delhi, 10 December
Each of these five days has included a few hours working quietly alone in this room, as the composition starts to take shape, in watercolour or acrylic. Sheikh and me stand to one side, with Bhupen hovering above us. The setting is Bombay (where Bhupen grew up), with the skyscrapers of Malabar Hill rising above the curve of Chowpatty Beach.

When I cross the vast city to friends' homes, it isn't always easy to combine drawing with eating together, viewing their work, catching up. As I stare at Vivan, keeping my pencil earnestly on the move, I hear Geeta exclaim, 'It's so *SWEET*' – my archaic practice in the era of the digital! Dismayingly, when Geeta sits here

AMIT AMBALAL IN
THE CAR, AHMEDABAD
Timothy Hyman
Pencil on paper
200 x 320mm
(7⁷⁄₈ x 12⁵⁄₈")

for a small painted sketch, it fails. After she's left, I try
a different tack – juxtaposing a head against a local
monument (as Albrecht Dürer did in his 1520 sketchbook
of his Netherlandish journey). In this case, it's Geeta's
head against the beautiful Lodi Tombs, five minutes
walk from here. Today I enjoyed a last sitting from Ranbir
Kaleka, back from Chicago. In the new, booming Indian
artworld he's emerged as an outstanding video master,
exhibiting internationally. Ranbir won't be in the group
portrait, but I wanted to make a drawing. Repeatedly,
my experience is of each friendship being reignited
through the pencil.

Ahmedabad, 14 December
The Gujarati metropolis was Bhupen's favourite city –
off the tourist track, but full of wonderful things to see.
In 1987 Judith and I were based here for three months
as guests of Raksha and Amit, in a separate house
that has become his studio. After lunch, I revisit the
majestic brick-built campus, masterpiece of the
American architect Louis Kahn, and make some
drawings. That evening and the next day I paint in a
little notebook, juxtaposing it against Amit's massive
profile, which I always think of as 'Chief Sitting Bull'.
I draw him repeatedly in the car on the way to the
Calico Museum.

Baroda, 21 December

Bhupen worked most of his life here, and I did several stints at the art school. When I first came to Baroda in 1981, Bhupen spoke of his delight in Nilima's profile (the only female portrait he ever made), while his closest lifelong comrade was Sheikh. Sheikh and Nilima have brewed up an ambitious plan – the three of us will travel together to the beautiful but remote fortress-city of Jaisalmer, an eighteen-hour journey. On his previous visit alongside Bhupen forty-four years earlier, Sheikh wrote some of his best-known Gujarati poems. Jaisalmer was then unknown, without a single hotel. Today we have marvellous rooms high in the walls, looking out over the city. My instinct is to stay put and draw, but Sheikh, even at seventy, is an indefatigable sightseer. At the end of an exhausting day, when I long for a cup of tea beside the calm lake, Sheikh insists on a boat ride. My grumbling turns to delight as I draw them both afloat. (A watercolour results the following day, as well as a small acrylic panel.)

Bombay, 27 December

Thrilled as ever by the sweep of Marine Drive, or the slice of it glimpsed from my art deco balcony here at the Sea Green Hotel. The Bombay setting has now come into focus. I ventured one evening to draw on the beach, pestered by small children and head-masseurs. I've also made a pastel of Sudhir and tracked down Atul, in the distant suburb where he's transformed his family *chawl* (tenement building) into a beautiful studio complex. In between, I've drawn or visited other old friends – Gieve Patel, Foy Nissen, the Sabavalas – and sensed our ageing. We all now wear glasses, and most of us are white-haired. It will be a sunset group.

SHEIKH AND NILIMA
AFLOAT, JAISALMER
Timothy Hyman
Acrylic on board
310 x 290mm
(12¹/₄ x 11³/₈")

Making so many portrait drawings (more in three weeks than I'd usually complete in a year) clarified what I was seeking – a kind of icon, nearer to mask than to straight representation; to uncover the mask beneath the social mask, cousin to caricature but more than merely comic.

On returning to London, I'm now at work on a 2-metre canvas that brings together eight friends as well as Bhupen and myself. (The Indian art circle that I was part of was larger, but you can only fit so many in.) I hope the eventual picture will convey my sense of a community of friendship.

This journey turned out to be a way of reopening a door – of re-entering a world that once seemed lost to me.

AROUND BHUPEN
Timothy Hyman
Acrylic on board
200 x 320mm
(7⁷⁄₈ x 12⁵⁄₈")

BHUPEN KHAKHAR (1934–2003) (above)
The best-known Indian painter of his generation.

(from left to right)
TIMOTHY HYMAN (b.1946)

GULAM MOHAMMED SHEIKH (b.1937)
Painter and poet, also working digitally.

VIVAN SUNDARAM (b.1943)
India's leading avant-garde artist.

GEETA KAPUR (b.1944)
Critic and curator.

DILLU (MRNALINI) MUKHERJEE (b.1947)
Sculptor.

SUDHIR PATWARDHAN (b.1949)
Painter and radiologist.

AMIT AMBALAL (b.1943)
Painter.

NILIMA SHEIKH (b.1945) (lower right)
Painter.

ATUL DODIYA (b.1959) (upper right)
The most prominent Indian painter of his generation.

PUIJO
Gareth Reid
Oil on board
355 x 380mm
(14 x 15")

In December I toured Finland for three weeks, taking in Helsinki, Oulu, Kajaani, Kuopio, Jyväskylä, Tampere and Turku. I visited 'winter-swimming clubs' in each of those places, where thousands of members swim in bitterly cold *avannot* (ice-holes) in otherwise frozen lakes and rivers. I was interested in the bond between bathers and the northern landscape, the incongruity of bare flesh and ice, and the stoic pursuit of invigoration through exposure to extremes in the near-constant dusk.

AVANTO
Gareth Reid

Oulu, 4 December
Mariia takes me to her club beside the river – a clubhouse, which looks closed up and shuttered, and then a hut for changing, closer to the water. It is frozen over, apart from an area kept unfrozen by pumps moving the water to the left of a jetty. It's 10pm, dark and minus 10 $^{\circ}$C – truly Arctic conditions. A man exits the hut as we're standing there, looking at the black water. He's young, skinny – and wearing speedos. Obviously I knew this went on, but still I'm not prepared for it. He quite literally goes for a swim for about thirty seconds, which seems like an eternity. I'm shocked; Mariia laughs at my shock. He does it seven days a week.

Oulu, 5 December
It is assumed at some stage today that I too will be swimming. It gets discussed. Mariia suggests I go with Timo to his town, Ii, forty km away, to a remote ice-hole with no warm showers or facilities nearby, and take the plunge with him. I try to make excuses. They go unheeded – this is the only time Timo can do it. I feel queasy. I say I have no gear with me. He says he'll lend me some speedos. I feel queasier. But I agree, pretending this isn't all utterly wrong. We go to Mariia's work where she presents me with a company towel and hat to use in Ii.

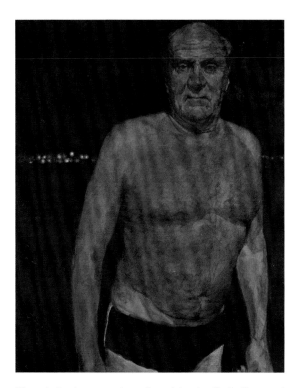

KAJAANI I
Gareth Reid
Oil on board
608 x 483mm
(23⁷/₈ x 19")

Timo (who is a great guy) and I set off. Coffee and fresh buns at his home, then on to the remote ice-hole. I get changed in a tiny riverside hut into a pair of someone else's old, baggy trunks and prime Timo on how to work the camera, then take the long walk down ice-covered steps towards a black, freezing abyss, camera bulb flashing. I am genuinely worried about having a heart attack, and we seem miles from medical help. But there's no getting out of it at this late stage. Timo says 'Remember to breathe'. I say 'Okay. Do I just go straight in?' I'm stalling, and not quite believing what is happening. Feet first, I dunk myself up to my neck for literally a second. And it's not too bad; then it feels really good and exhilarating. I feel excited and full of energy and tingly, almost uncomfortably so. Friends and family get phoned.

Oulu, 7 December

A burly, older guy comes out of the changing room. I mime taking a photo, but he says, 'No take', dips his toe in and said, 'Cold'. He lowers himself in halfway, then, a bit surprised, says 'Not cold'. It *is* cold. The technique is usually to go straight in, without fuss and mostly silently. Mariia does it serenely, smiling continuously, which contrasts well with my panicky, flustered blowing. Some just dip themselves to their necks, then out. Some have a brief paddle, others a more prolonged swim. Today I witness the first screaming by a duo of ladies I would have assumed to be stoic, and then the longest time in the water, first by an old woman, and then by a taciturn man who not only smashes her already impressive record but actually swims under water – head submerged – which is usually a no-no.

TAMPERE I
Gareth Reid
Acrylic on board
380 x 330mm
(15 x 13")

Kuopio, 10 December

We go to another place that has a sauna. Everyone here is doing the sauna/avanto/sauna, multiple times. They're mostly older ladies (one is eighty). With Anita interpreting, I'm allowed to take a lot of pictures. One man had heart surgery last week, scars and all – and there was me worrying about heart failure. I then go for a sauna. It's mixed, with about ten older, sturdy ladies, Jouko and me crammed into a small, boiling wooden cube. Very convivial atmosphere with a lot of laughing (in my direction) and chatting. Jouko is clearly a ladies' man and holds court, looking like a tanned Viking. He's just been to Thailand, he showed me his tan-line. This time I go from sauna to water three times, staying in a bit longer each time and as a result feel much happier about everything. This is clearly a big reason that this is so popular here – it helps people get through the depression of the dark winter period. Even the longest swim lasts only minutes, which, as a hobby, makes it accessible to even the busiest on a daily basis.

Tampere, 14 December
We drive to the edge of one of Tampere's two massive lakes. There are waves. A beautiful spot and a big club. Is this the 'blister club' I'd heard about? The sauna is huge (sixty people capacity), brightly lit and wood-fired. Tier upon tier of perspiring men and women, lobster-red, super-blotchy, enduring the temperature and loving it. The softly spoken academic who collects me turns out to be the hardened heat junkie. It can't be hot enough for her in there. I come close to passing out. Breathing is painful – you instinctively want to cover your mouth due to the inhaled heat – but the smaller the aperture, the more searingly hot your lips become. There's authentic birch whipping. Everyone is wearing *pipas* (beanie hats) to stop their hair from burning. My hostess shows me the thermometer. Only 114 $^\circ$C tonight. Sometimes it's up to 130 $^\circ$/140 $^\circ$C. They've slow-baked a ham in there. Icy water seems like deliverance.

Tampere, 15 December
The steam coming off these guys is comic. They're engulfed in it as they emerge, mottled vermillion, into the cold. I've never seen blotchiness like it. It's very busy and there is a conveyor belt/escalator feel to the long steps. The water is illuminated from beneath. It's all very nice. And you can buy beer and sausages to grill outside as well, which clearly adds to the whole event. These people are hardcore. Most have been here for ages – fire, ice, fire, ice etc. etc. The top tier inside the sauna at Tampere is unbearably hot. There are folk up there sitting right next to the furnace, lashing water onto the coals, having to shield their faces from the heat. They are in pain, hunched over, grimacing, shielding, and are as red and sweaty as any human being I've ever seen (and that includes myself after a short jog). You feel really good and invigorated afterwards, but this does seem rather extreme.

PICTURE CREDITS

ACKNOWLEDGEMENTS

I would like to thank all the artists who submitted for the 2008 Award and to offer congratulations to the winner of the prize for a younger painter, as well as to the three shortlisted artists within the overall submission.

I am very grateful to the diligent and hard-working judges for this year's BP Portrait Award – Sadie Coles, David Mach, Corinne Miller and Des Violaris. My thanks also go to Sarah Howgate, Contemporary Curator, for her work on the exhibition and for selecting the BP Travel Award with Liz Rideal and Des Volaris. I would like to offer particular thanks to Alexander McCall Smith for his delightful catalogue essay, which makes intriguing connections between fiction and depiction. I am also grateful to Claudia Bloch for her editorial work, Anne Sørensen for designing the catalogue and to Flora Fricker for managing the 2008 BP Portrait Award exhibition so capably. My thanks also go to Pim Baxter, Andrea Easey, Denise Dean, Denise Ellitson, Neil Evans, Ian Gardner, Sumi Ghose, Michelle Greaves, Celia Joicey, Ruth Müller-Wirth, Jonathan Rowbotham, Jude Simmons, Liz Smith, Sarah Tinsley and other colleagues at the National Portrait Gallery for all their hard work in making the project such a continuing success. My thanks also go to the white wall company for their contribution during the selection and judging process.

SANDY NAIRNE
Director, National Portrait Gallery

INDEX

Figures in *italics* refer to illustrations.